# THE PENISTONE SCENE

***Captured in photographs over the years***

*Compiled by*
**R.N. Brownhill**

*Assisted by*
**J. Smethurst**

*R.N. Brownhill*

*J.Smethurst*

BRIDGE PUBLICATIONS
PENISTONE · ENGLAND

*Bridge Publications*
*2 Bridge Street, Penistone*
*Sheffield S30 6AJ*



*First Published 1987*



*British Library Cataloguing in Publication Data*

Brownhill, R.N.
The Penistone scene.
1. Penistone (South Yorkshire) – History – Pictorial works 2. Penistone (South Yorkshire) – Description – Views
I. Title
942.8'25 DA690.P3

ISBN 0-947934-16-2
ISBN 0-947934-15-4 Pbk

*Printed and Bound in Great Britain by*
*Whitstable Litho Ltd., Whitstable, Kent*

## Acknowledgement

I wish to thank all the many people who have provided general information to make this publication possible, and the following for the loan of photographs:

Mr J. Smethurst
Mr G. Knowles
Mr D. Roebuck
Mr G.D. Lindley
Mrs M. Marsh
Mr J. Illingworth
Mr D. Sanderson
Mr J. Penney
Mr G. Wood
Mrs E. Hoyland
Miss V. Nicholson
Mrs D. Cartwright
Mrs L. Moorhouse
Mrs M. Haigh
Mr K. Peel
Mr G. Scarfe

# Introduction

Penistone, at 747 feet above sea level, is still a market town, as the influx of farmers from the surrounding district every Thursday clearly shows.

The agricultural show on a Saturday in September, but formerly the Thursday of Barnsley Feast Week, completes the farmers' yearly cycle. The Penistone breed of sheep has staged a revival in recent years and can be seen at the show. The Annual Fair and Sing, now in its 102nd year, takes place on the first Sunday after the 24th June, and the Ploughing Association continues to have annual matches, with the first recorded one taking place in 1884. At 11 o'clock on Shrove Tuesday morning the Pancake Bell is rung and in olden times was the signal for the apprentices to down tools for the rest of the day.

The ancient church of St John the Baptist, steeped in history over many centuries, has been well documented during recent years. Sadly the Netherfield Chapel is no longer in use and the congregation have amalgamated with St Paul's to form St Andrew's, whose new chapel building is in course of construction on the site of the Wesleyan Chapel in High Street. The former New Connexion chapel building has recently been extended to give extra facilities for the clinic, but the Bullhouse chapel still retains its religious simplicity and continues to thrive after almost three centuries. This year is the first time since last century that the procession of witness by the local Church and Chapels has not taken place at Whitsuntide between Thurlstone and Penistone.

The Grammar School, founded in 1392, is almost as old as Winchester College, founded in 1382 and reputed to be one of the oldest public schools in England.

The elderly of the district are well catered for with

*Penistone Church*

modern accommodation at Green Park House and Pendon House, which is in extreme contrast to the gaunt stone buildings of the almshouses at Hoylandswaine or the workhouse at Netherfields.

The area supports a varied assortment of sports and pastimes including football, cricket, tennis, bowls, opera, brass band, handbells, plays, male voice and combined choirs, Guides and Scouts, and men's and women's amenity groups. Combined with glorious scenery, and many bridle paths and pathways with which to explore the area on foot, these all add up to make Penistone a pleasant area to live in if you can come to terms with the winds, ice and snow during the winter time.

## PENISTONE *as seen by Revd John Aldom in 1886:*

PENISTONE! dear Penistone!
 Thy name falls on my ear,
And calls up mem'ries of my own,
 Far back, and yet so dear,
Dear! yes! so dear, they'll ever last,
But cast a shadow on the past.

It was when life was young and bright
 I first gazed on thy hills,
And oh! how lovely was the sight,
 And sweet the murmuring rills;
So different from the Cutler's town,
On which the smoking chimnies frown.

And soon I left my Sheffield home,
 Thy brighter scenes to greet
'Midst hills and valleys I could roam,
 From Sheffield's dusty street;
And friendships formed I can't forget,
They're wreathed with ever-greens as yet.

The Vicar, too, so good and kind,
 With ever beaming face,
Impressed himself upon my mind,
 As 'full of truth and grace.'
His corpse I brought in death so pale,
From Rowsley, near to Chatsworth Vale.

And then with many tears and sighs,
 We laid him in the ground,
Until the angel from the skies
 Pours forth the trumpet sound,
'Arise ye dead,' and come ye blest
'And with the Saviour ever rest.'

As years rolled on, I tarried still
 With those I'd learnt to love,
And pointed, too, to Zion's hill,
 To realms of bliss above.
Oh! it is sweet to think of those
Who sleep with Christ in deep repose.

The Grammar School, where through the day,
 I taught the village youth,
And tried to guide them in the ways
 Of virtue and of truth:
Hail! ancient seat of wisdom's lore,
Oh! may'st thou prosper evermore.

And see! the stone above the door!
 'Disce aut discede's' wrought,
Which strikes the eye yet more and more,
 And leads the mind to thought,
'Learn or depart,' it means to say,
And do not waste your youthful day.

I pause, look back upon the years
 Now gone, for ever gone;
My eyes will fill with mournful tears,
 As ever and anon
I see, around in memory's light,
The loved who've passed from earthly sight.

REV. JOHN W. ALDOM, M.A.

# THE CHURCH

1964: before the alteration of choir stalls etc and installation of the new organ.

The Church is without doubt the most ancient and beautiful building in Penistone, dominating as it has done for centuries the town and surrounding countryside.

The history of the building of Penistone Church is as follows. The nave and chancel along with the pillars and arches, with the exception of the last sixteen feet at the east end, was built at the end of the 12th century. It was extended 200 years later.

The original roof was high pitched like an inverted 'V'. This was replaced later, the walls being raised at the same time. Given a close look, this can be clearly seen.

The tower was built about the year 1500. The font is ancient but the font cover, benches, panelling and screen were added in 1956, a gift of Mr Hawley.

The tower and the church are built of local stone. The tower, containing a ringing chamber, clockroom and bell chamber, is 80 feet high. In the bell chamber are many records of peals rung, and boards recording the various charities belonging to the church and the legacies that founded them.

On the 3rd September 1822 Robert Bramall, aged 73 years, was killed by overturning the tenor bell. He endeavoured to hold the rope and was raised from the floor five or six yards, then fell with such force that he only lived a few days. He had been sexton for over twenty years.

*Nave, Chancel and East Window*

*Nave, Baptistry and West Window*

The porch on the south side was built in the 18th century with the stone from the ruined chantry chapel of St John, which was on the road to Hartcliffe called Chapel Lane. The gravestones from the chapel make up the porch seats.

The church at one time was filled with box pews, with a three decker pulpit standing against the second pillar from the front at the south side. A gallery under the tower extended into the nave, serving also as the organ loft.

Canon Turnbull removed the pulpit, pews and gallery in 1862, replacing them with the present day ones.

There are ten pillars plus four half pillars in the church, making twelve in all. One of them, easily recognized, is different from the rest and is known as the Judas Pillar. On the North Side of the building a carved stone is set into a pillar. This is believed to be the shaft of a Saxon Cross, probably a local preaching cross used before the church was built.

There are many memorials and gravestones in the church; these include the Bosville and West families' – also one which commemorates Nicholas Saunderson, who was blind and became Professor of Mathematics at Cambridge.

The only ancient glass is a beautiful enamelled window in the South Clerestory containing a coat of arms of the Bosville family, and dates from the 17th century.

Six large windows have been installed in this century, the names of the donors and the dates can be clearly seen.

The weather vane on top of the tower in the shape of a fish was made in stainless steel in 1975 by a Penistone pensioner. The early Christians used the fish as a secret sign pledging the Catholic faith in code, the letters of the Greek word for a fish signifying Jesus Christ, God's Son, Saviour.

Before the fish the weather vane was in the shape of an arrow.

In 1643, during the Civil War, the church was garrisoned by the Parliamentarian troops under the command of Captain Rich of Bullhouse, Captain Adam Eyre of Hazlehead and Captain Shirt of Cawthorne. A canon was placed there to defend the town against the Royalists commanded by Sir Francis Wortley and Sir Thomas Wentworth of Bretton. It was while on lookout on top of the church that a sentry was shot by a sniper.

Many interesting books have been published about Penistone church; a brief history and guide currently obtainable contains many fascinating facts and dates for the visitor.

On a buttress to the east of the south door is carved a mediaeval sun dial used before the clock was installed. The markings are not to indicate the time but to inform the populace of the time of Mass.

*Church sundial*

*Church plate*

Pictured are two silver chalices with covers. One bears the inscription: 'The gift of the Lady Mary Beaumont eldest daughter of George Burdet Esq. of Denby Hall A.D. 1673'. The hallmark is of the same date. They weigh 11 and 10 ounces. Also a silver flagon of an earlier date weighing 55 ounces and a silver paten weighing 21 ounces given by Mrs Bosville of Gunthwaite.

Resting on the outside of the east end of the church is the gravestone of Molyneaux Bunny, who served with reputation in the armies of King William and Queen Anne and was a gentleman born; he must have served under the Duke of Marlborough. He died on 6th May 1749.

*Molyneaux Bunny's gravestone*

# TOWN CENTRE

Penistone Church, 1905 – Restoration: New pinnacles on top of the tower were erected. Two of the old ones can still be seen in the churchyard. Gates which once stretched across the top of Shrewsbury Road can be observed in the bottom right hand corner of the picture.

*Penistone Church, 1905*

*Cloth Hall, c.1910*

In 1763 a cloth hall and shambles was built at Penistone by Josias Wordsworth at a cost of £800. Previously a room over the old Grammar School had been used, but the cloth market was never very considerable and the purpose-built hall was soon turned to other uses. Some of these were: Post Office, White Bear Inn, Hunters grocery stores, British Legion Club etc., the whole building finally becoming A.M. Clark's Chemist's shop. In 1825 the entire block was sold for £615, and in 1903 the same block was sold for £4,400. On the 1749 map of Penistone it is situated in the beast market on the place named 'sheds'.

*Cloth Hall, 1949*

*Grammar School from churchyard, c.1890*

The old Penistone Grammar School c.1890. This school stood on the site of the present day Midland Bank Buildings. Demolished in 1893, the Grammar School moved to Weirfield near to the present school. It was held at one time in the south aisle of the church. The picture taken from inside the churchyard shows two lamps where the lych gate stands today. The other picture is taken from in front of the Cloth Hall. Previous to 1763 the Cloth Hall was in a room over the Grammar School.

*Grammar School and shop from Cloth Hall, c.1890*

The clock fitted on Easter Sunday, 10th April 1817 has only one face. The two huts on the site of the present day bus shelter were G. Ashworth's (barbers) and A. Heeley's (greengrocers). Swallow's hairdresser, now in the Old Commercial Inn, was under the barber's pole (bottom centre) and the White Bear under the flagpole.

*Town Centre, c.1900*

*Town Centre, 1987*

*Market Place, c.1894*

Bradley's sweet shop, Hudson & Birks boot and shoe warehouse, and the cottages on the right were demolished to build the National Provincial Bank, now the National Westminster Bank, which was opened on 2nd November 1931. The three storey building was the Commercial Inn. The Post Office was situated in the Midland Bank Buildings opened in 1895 and closed October 1938. The sign under the lamp on the corner of the Cloth Hall advertises Pratts petrol. A.M. Clark's claim to be the first establishment to sell petrol to the motorist in Penistone.

*Market Place, 1987*

*Unveiling of war memorial, 9th August 1924*

# MARKET STREET

18 Market Street as it was in the last century. R.D. Woodcock erected the building in two stages. The first stage, as shown in the picture, involved moving his merchandise into the rear. The front half was then erected without the loss of a day's business. When the building became too large for their requirements, Woodcocks moved down the road to number 10, formerly Walkers' confectioners and F. Brownhill's butchers. Besides being ironmongers, Woodcocks were also locksmiths. Note key over name.

*Woodcock's (original building)*

*R.D. Woodcock/Walkers, 1972*

*Market Street, c.1894*

*The market was held in the street; granted originally by Godfrey Bosville of Gunthwaite Hall in 1699.*

*Hunters Tea Store, c.1900. Now the entrance to A.M. Clark's Chemist's. Note the bacon hung outside alongside the basket chairs, priced 1s.0d (5p).*

*Side of J. Parkin's property*

One of the oldest buildings in Penistone, formerly John Parkin's house (now occupied by K. Beever, greengrocer), was built in 1726. The Fieldsend family inhabited it for over 70 years as a shop of various sorts. The stone on the north west corner with 'P' and other letters in addition to the date would probably show the extent of Parkin's boundary. On the north side of the building are three pillars. A local theory is that this is most likely the old entrance, facing as it would be the old beast market before the Cloth Hall was built.

*Old map*

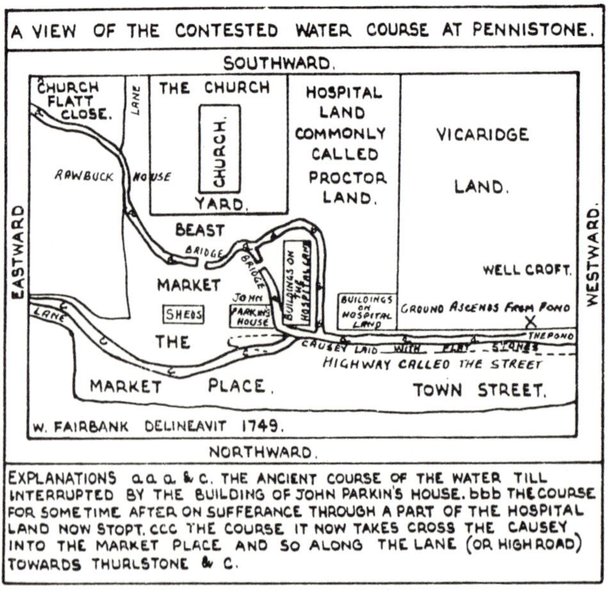

PENISTONE IN 1749.

*John Parkin's stone*

*Market Street (Dr Ross area), c.1900*

Market Street, west side. The house on the left of the picture, now demolished, was the residence of the late Dr Ross. The Co-op now occupies the site.

*Market Street, shops on east side (GT News area)*

Market Street, east side. The first four shops were built in 1852 by J.F. Moorhouse (for Mrs Calvert who lived in the first shop) where previously stood the Sportsman's Arms, next to which stood three cottages. One of the occupants of these was George Bramall, a blacksmith who had his shop adjoining the cottage in which he lived.

# HIGH STREET

*High Street shops on east side, c.1895 (Showing cottages now replaced by shops shown in 1987 picture)*

*High Street shops on east side, 1987*

*High Street on east side, c.1905*

The gentleman in the doorway is called Washington, Piano Dealer, who also sold cloth etc. On the right is Hinchliff's milliners, while in the background, behind the horse and cart, are the premises of the first Co-op in Penistone.

*High Street on east side, 1987*

# HIGH STREET & THE GREEN

*High Street in library area, c.1930*

Originally called Pinfold Lane, leading as it did to a pinfold situated at the bottom of Cubley Hill. The rights of the pinfold were sold by PUDC on 11th November 1909, for £10, to Messrs Brook & Co of the Cubley Brook Brewery.

*Vinegar brewery from The Green, 1973 (formerly Messrs Brook & Co.; it was demolished in 1975 and replaced by houses.)*

# ST MARY'S STREET

*Old Commercial Inn (now occupied by hairdresser D. Swallow)*

The picture, taken c.1917, shows Mr Thomas Hinchliffe, owner of the B.T. Hinchliffe (his father) footwear and drapery store. Ensor's shop was later occupied by Mr Arthur Heeley, greengrocer, and at present by Mr J.G. Smith, housefurnisher from Thurlstone. (see p.60)

*B.T. Hinchliffe*

*Old lock-up, 1965. General view*

*Old lock-up, 1965. Interior with W. Penistone.*

The town jail or lock-up (as shown on 1854 map). The late Mr J. W. Penistone, photographed in the lockup in 1965, remembered it being used by the police to detain a violent drunken man early in this century. To the right hand side of the door, and behind the window opening, was a small room with a stone sink and a stone staircase which led up to the constable's lodgings. In previous times there was a notice outside the lock-up, stating 'Relatives of prisoners can buy fresh straw at 2d per bundle.'

*Market, c.1910. The small wooden shed with the flap raised was at one time Todkill's greengrocers.*

*Mart and Goods Station, c.1910*

Hanson's Auction Mart was a market built over the other side of the wall to replace the street market. It was a failure owing to the fact that the farmers had to pay to use it, the street trading being free. In the background is Penistone's first railway station, built c.1846, later a goods yard, eventually replaced by the present station.

# BRIDGE STREET

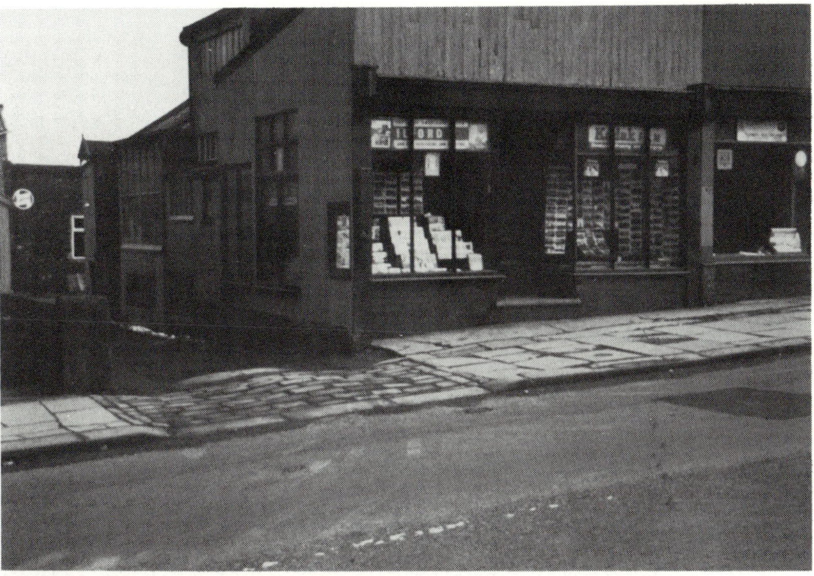

***Biltcliffe's Photo Shop and Studio, taken in 1964, just prior to closing.***

*Bridge Hotel and Black Swan*

The Landlord, Mr Charles Gillis (in the doorway of the Bridge Hotel) was there from 1924 until 1932 before moving to the Spread Eagle Hotel. During his time it was the main meeting place of the navvies during the construction of the Scout Dike reservoir. The adjoining building was originally the Black Swan Inn, replaced in 1866 by the Bridge Hotel, which was built by Amos Green, the local blacksmith.

Sanderson's Bridge End Garage was founded in 1885 by Mr Joseph Penn. As the photograph of c.1922 shows, it was then J. Penn's cycle works, but by 1924 had been changed to Penistone Motor and Cycle Engineering Works. Shown from left to right are: Fred Biltcliffe, Ernest Mitchell Sanderson (owner), Harry Mackenzie, Leonard Sanderson (son), Jack Thornton and Bernard Tomlinson. (Note: the greengrocer with his horse and dray came from Sheffield and was known as 'Sheffield Jack'.)

*J. Penn's, c.1922*

*J. Penn and Robinson's, c.1924*

*Bridge Street taken from Netherfield showing Whiteley's Rug Mill on the left by the tree. Their other premises were in Talbot Road. (Note: the present Sanderson's garage had not been built.)*

# CHURCH STREET

*National School tablet*

The tablet on the wall of the National School records that in 1822 Mr Joseph Camm, born in Penistone but residing in Beverley, endowed £400 towards the building of a girls' school which was built by public subscription and opened in January 1823. In 1827 there were 120 pupils.

*Church Hill and viaduct from top of church, c.1910. Not much has changed except the housing estate west of the viaduct.*

*Church Hill from railway banking, c.1910. The four shops on the left and the Town Hall were not yet built.*

*Railway Terrace, with Cammell Laird's in full production. (Both now demolished.)*

*The Old Hearse House at the bottom of the churchyard in Church Hill.*

*Aaron Shore's draper's shop, Church Street, 1956 (now flats)*

# SHREWSBURY ROAD

*Saturday night market produce at top of road, c.1891. In 1891 markets were held in the Market Place on Saturday afternoons and evenings, as shown in the picture.*

*Top of road, 1987. The bus shelter was built in 1936.*

The Town Hall was opened on 31st October 1914, being a continuation of the free library. The cost of the hall and the council offices was about £4,000. For many years a building originally erected as a gas fitting showroom did service as a public hall. It was situated on Stottercliffe and known as the Assembly Rooms. It later became a picture palace and was destroyed by fire in 1923.

*The Town Hall, 1987*

*Assembly Rooms*

*Salvation Army and Conservative office, c.1910*

The Conservative offices are now a baker's shop. The two-storey wooden construction was the Salvation Army building, while Eastmans Limited were butchers. The shop, now a 'chippy', was Fowler's greengrocers.

*and in 1987*

# PERSONALITIES

*J.N. Dransfield*

## *Canon W.S. Turnbull*

William Turnbull was Parish Priest at Penistone from 1855 until his death in 1913. He was elected to the chairmanship of the Penistone Local Board (formed in 1869) and its successor The Penistone Urban District Council for at least 37 years. Among other achievements he founded the Farm Chapel at Snowden Hill.

## *John Ness Dransfield*

John Ness Dransfield, the son of John Dransfield, solicitor, Penistone, was born at Green House in Penistone on 26th October 1839. He commenced his education at Penistone Grammar School, finishing up at Windermere College in 1855. After passing his examinations as a solicitor he joined his father's firm, which became Dransfield & Son. He later was a partner of Colonel Charles Hodgkinson in the firm of Dransfield & Hodgkinson, which is still practising in Penistone. He retired in 1892. In 1906 he published *The History of Penistone,* a much sought after and prized book to the present day. To him we owe a debt of gratitude for much of the past history, facts and figures that can be obtained from his book. He was also Secretary of Penistone Agricultural Show almost continuously from 1866 to 1883. A keen huntsman, he was connected with the Penistone Hunt for 80 years. He died on Sunday, 13th July 1930, aged 90 years, and is buried in Penistone cemetery.

*Canon William Stephenson Turnbull*

## *James Ashton*

James Ashton (nicknamed 'pot-oil') was verger and town crier. The bell is in the possession of Mr R. Woodcock. It was reported that he left it with the landlord of a local inn and disappeared forever on the moors. He lived in Fieldsend's Yard.

*James Ashton (1887-        )*

## OYEZ!

I'm leaving the place up yonder:
The House on Netherfield Hill -
I have lived the life of a freeman:
Of such charity I'll speak no ill

These are the words of Jim Pothoil:
A worthy of Penistone Town —
Whose whimsical cry, bell and tale
Gave rise to sneer, laugh and frown.

Just a peep at Jim in his glory:
Uniform slashed with rich gold -
His big toned bell loudly clanging:
He struts and a tale unfolds.

Came the day when he faced the long journey:
Away to the great beyond -
I must finish my days in my country
The place where I really belong.

Away out on the wide open moorland:
James Ashton was wending his way -
Tired, bewildered, tottering forward,
On this the last of his days.

In a vast and lonely silence:
He lies in a kingly tomb -
With a shroud of purple heather,
And harebells ringing him through.

James Lees

*Joshua Biltcliffe*

## *Joshua and John Thomas Biltcliffe*

Joshua Biltcliffe, founder of the photographic studios at Bridge Street, Penistone, started his career in a small hut at The Prospect, Thurlstone. This was later brought by horse and cart to become the studio part of the Penistone building. The showroom, picture frame workshop and darkroom were added, and the business became firmly established. More shops were then opened at Denby Dale and Skelmanthorpe, and his two sons, Fred and John Thomas, joined the firm. Fred later took over Skelmanthorpe and John Thomas acquired Penistone. To Joshua and John Thomas Biltcliffe the town of Penistone is deeply indebted for the many old photographs we possess and for the historical knowledge they provide. Many of the photographs in this book were taken by them, and it is our hope that it will help preserve them for future generations. Joshua died in 1937, aged 85 years. His son John Thomas died in 1964 aged 84 years, after which the business closed down, the shop later being dismantled to make way for a garage entrance.

*John Thomas Biltcliffe*

## *J.W. Penistone*

Joseph William Penistone (1888-1976) was the eldest son of Mr & Mrs George Henry Penistone, who were Cook and Gardener to the late Canon Turnbull. Attending St John's Church of England School under Mr Herbert Jordan, he passed the County Minor Scholarship when 11 years old and then moved to Penistone Grammar School for four years with a maintenance grant of £5 paid when he left. In his period at the Grammar School he passed the Cambridge Junior Examination with third class honours.

The only school uniform in those days was a cap which cost sixpence. As a reward for passing the scholarship his mother bought him an American Organ, which Mr Jordan taught him to play. Afterwards he played at Canon Turnbull's church services at Midhope and Langsett, transporting the organ by Bailey's horse-drawn cab. He later became a Sunday School teacher, after which he was made Sunday School Secretary and then Sunday School Superintendant.

On leaving the Grammar School in 1904 he became a junior clerk at Dransfield & Hodgkinson's, and it was in this period that he made a complete record of the gravestones in Penistone churchyard, a record that can still be seen in Penistone Library. John Ness Dransfield presented him with an original copy of *The History of Penistone* for his efforts.

Pursuing his local interests he became secretary of Penistone Church Football Club and Penistone Church Cricket Club, and was also a member of the Penistone Sing Committee. After many years as a local newspaper reporter and serving as a political agent for the Conservative and Liberal Parties, he retired and wrote what he will be best remembered for, which was a long series of articles published weekly in a local newspaper under the heading of 'Bygones of Penistone', containing many items of interest. He also gave considerable assistance in the production of the book *The Further History of Penistone*. When he reached the ripe old age of 83 years he decided he had written enough and retired.

*J.W. Penistone*

## *James H. Wood*

James H. Wood was a well-known Penistone historian. He produced *The Penistone Almanack* for many years, was a leading figure in the staging of Penistone Show, and the owner of the Don Press. He died on the 21st October 1951 aged 86 years.

*James H. Wood*

*Professor N. Saunderson*

# *Professor N. Saunderson*

Professor Nicholas Saunderson, a famous old boy of Penistone Grammar School, was born in Thurlstone in 1682. When he was about a year old he lost his sight through contracting smallpox. Tradition has it that he taught himself to read by passing his fingers over the gravestones in the churchyard. It is interesting to note that this was 150 years before Braille was invented. A great friend of Sir Isaac Newton, Nicholas was appointed a Professor of Mathematics in 1711 and lectured at Cambridge. He died at the age of 57 years on 19th April 1739 and is buried at Boxworth. The stone now set in the wall of the annexe of the old Town End School playground at Thurlstone came from a building on the site of the cottage where he was born.

# *A.R. Lee*

A cornerstone of community life in Penistone, the late Arthur Robert Lee, affectionately known as 'Spinner', was awarded the British Empire Medal in recognition of his 40 years' service as a part-time fireman. He was chairman of the Penistone and District Operatic Society and was associated with Penistone Church Football Club for over 50 years. He died on 24th October 1982, aged 73 years.

*A.R. Lee, B.E.M.*

## *E.E. Worsfold*

Renowned for his exceptional strength, Ernest E. Worsfold was well known locally, working as a parcel porter on Penistone Railway Station. He was very experienced in the art of carrying parcels etc. on his head. Sometimes objects of great weight were transported to customers by this method, usually, almost unbelievably, whilst riding his bicycle. A non-smoker and teetotaller, he died at the age of 70 in 1954.

*E.E. Worsfold*

*J.W. Mellor*

## *J.W. Mellor*

Mr John William Mellor lost his arm during the first world war and worked at William Gittus & Son Ltd., railway wagon repairers. He was the 2nd team captain of the Yorkshire Steel & Iron Works Cricket Club, established 1867 (now Penistone C.C.), which won the championship of the Chapeltown League in 1935. He used a specially weighted bat and was a close-to-the wicket fielder.

*J. Taylor, blacksmith, at the anvil in the 'Smithy' at Bridge End.*

In 1921 Fred Taylor, father of John, took over the blacksmith's shop from Enoch Roebuck. In 1947 John became a partner in the firm, taking full control 10 years later on the death of his father. His proud boast, made with a twinkle in his eye, is that everything produced is 'Taylor made'.

*John and Mary Brownhill: 'Mine hosts' of the Wentworth Arms, c.1890. Also butchers in Market Street and Spring Vale.*

**There are many other local personalities, but photographs are not available.**

# PLACES OF WORSHIP

## *Bullhouse Chapel*

*Bullhouse Chapel (exterior)*

Bullhouse chapel was built for Protestant Dissenters with firm Puritan beliefs who were unhappy with the way of worship at the church. The datestone over the door gives its date of completion as 18th April 1692.

The gravestone of Elkanah Rich covered by a wooden floor at the south end of the chapel bears the

*Door*

*Datestone*

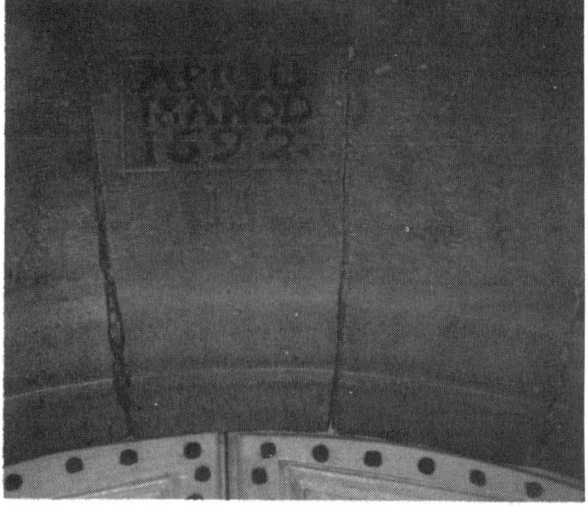

inscription, 'This building was erected by him in AD1692'.

It is said to be the oldest building in the country with a continuous history of non-conformist worship. The well-worn doorstep under the studded door gives some idea of the number of people that have passed through in the last 300 years. A window on the west side of the door shows the handywork of John Taylor, apprentice plumber and glazier, who etched his name and date on the pane in 1843.

*Engraving on window at Bullhouse*

*Bullhouse Chapel (interior)*

# *Netherfield Chapel*

*Netherfield Chapel (exterior)*

Netherfield Chapel, with its beautiful rose window, was built in 1788 following religious gatherings at the home of Mr William Moorhouse, a weaver who lived in Thurlstone.

Two of the founders were Joseph Moss, a tailor, of Penistone Green and his brother John who are recorded on a tablet on an inside wall.

In 1882 a new Sunday School and classrooms were added, and in 1902 a kitchen and Church Parlour completed the extensions.

A long-serving minister was the Revd Hywel, Jones who officiated from 1929 to 1950 and from 1960 to 1968. The Chapel was closed in April 1981 when it was incorporated into St Andrew's.

*Netherfield Chapel, 1965 (interior)*

*St Paul's Wesleyan Chapel*

## *St Paul's*

Built in 1872 at a cost of £1600, Penistone Wesleyan Chapel was demolished in 1986. Being quite spacious, it could seat 400 people, the basement providing accommodation for 200 children. This was the second chapel built by the Wesleyan body in Penistone. The first was erected in 1808 at a cost of £150, but with the increase in members brought about by the opening of the steel works, this became too small and was sold, being converted into two houses, 22 and 24 High Street. The windows can still be seen in the houses at the present time.

## *Tin Chapel, Springvale*

The 'Tin Chapel' was built c. 1860 following services which had been held in a cottage in Queen Street. The congregation was made up mainly of railway workers and their families and the 'Tin Chapel' was in use until the present chapel was built in 1926. The pitch pine pews were transferred to the new chapel and are still in use today.

*Tin Chapel, Springvale*

*Catholic Church*

## *St Mary's*

The Roman Catholic congregation have held their services at many places in the last 50 years. In 1941 a room above A.W. Heeley's greengrocer's, which is now J.T. Smith's, was used. In 1946 they moved to premises adjacent to the Rose and Crown, where they worshipped until moving to T.W. Ward's offices in Sheffield Road. In 1965, after a brief spell in St John's Community Centre, a new church, St Mary's, was built in Talbot Road and opened on 31st May by Bishop Dwyer of Leeds.

## *Thurlstone Providence*

In 1828 the chapel was in a workshop behind some cottages at the Top of the Town. The present one was built in 1867. Baptisms were performed in a little stream and later in the River Don.

*Thurlstone Providence Strict and Particular Baptist Chapel*

*Thurlstone Wesleyan*

## *Thurlstone Wesleyan*

Thurlstone Wesleyan Church was opened on 24th July 1889, services having been previously held at premises on 'The Green'. The last service was held on 26th May (Whit Sunday) 1985.

# THE RAILWAY

*Penistone Station (towards Huddersfield platform), c.1910*

*Barnsley Junction, c.1910*

An old stanchion on the Huddersfield platform of Penistone Station is a relic of the Manchester, Sheffield & Lincolnshire Railway Co., signified by the letters M.S.L.R. This stanchion is still in existence and can be seen by the visitor.

In the derailment picture a runaway wagon crashed into the Penistone goods station buffers and narrowly missed destroying an old Bridge Street landmark.

*Stanchion of Huddersfield line*

*Derailment at goods station*

*Viaduct disaster (engine)*

The viaduct which carries the Penistone to Huddersfield line over the River Don was built in 1849 by Messrs Ingham and Bower. The stone was obtained from the quarry behind Oxspring Wire Mill and was conveyed by a tramway along the riverside. There are 29 arches, including the bridge over the road. On 2nd February 1916, the second and third arches collapsed. An L. & Y. tank engine fell with the debris, later to be cut up and removed piecemeal. The line was reopened on 14th August 1916. A 'halt' station consisting of wooden platforms was built at Hoylandswaine road bridge and used during the reconstruction.

*Viaduct Collapse*

*Steps leading to Hoylandswaine bridge temporary station during repair of viaduct, 1916.*

*Ticket*

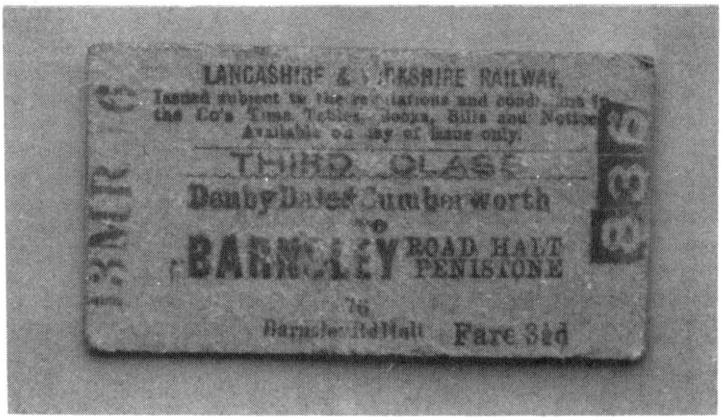

The Bullhouse disaster occurred at Bullhouse railway bridge on Wednesday, 16th July 1884, causing the deaths of 24 people and severely injuring 64 others. 19 were killed on the spot; 5 died later. The cause of the disaster was the engine's crank axle breaking and leaving the rails. The carriages went down the banking but the engine carried on down the track for 150 yards before coming to a halt. The engine driver and fireman were unhurt.

*Bullhouse railway disaster*

# STEELWORKS

*Cammell Laird's Old Side*

*Bessemer*

In 1862-3 Messrs Benson Adamson & Garnett erected an iron and steel works on a 22 acre site off Sheffield Road, to become known as the Old Side and nicknamed 'The Nibble'. The firm was purchased in May 1864 by Charles Cammell & Co., who produced Acid Bessemer Steel to make into ingots, rails, fishplates, railway axles and tyres etc. In 1917, now known as Cammell Laird & Co. Ltd., it was called upon by the wartime Government to increase the country's output of gun steel.

Forty acres of land was bought on the south of the railway, known later as 'The New Side'. The two halves of the works were connected by a subway under the main line railway. But sadly for Penistone, when in February 1930 Cammell Lairds joined the English Steel Corporation, the works were closed down to lessen the cost of production and to save transport. As many as 1500 men and boys had been employed there at one time.

The New Side was occupied in 1935 by David Brown's, who are still in production at the present time.

*Cammell Laird's Old Side, showing station before modernization*

*After modernization*

*Cammell Laird site. Old Side today from railway station*

*New Side, from railway*

*New Side, from road*

*David Brown's workforce, 1937*

# OXSPRING WIRE MILL

*Cottages*

Where the wiremill cottages are situated the Earl of Shrewsbury had a bloomery. It was here that iron to be supplied to Wortley Forge was extracted from iron ore obtained from Denby.

# *History of the foundation of Winterbottom (Wiredrawers) Ltd. (formerly G. Winterbottom & Co.)*

George Winterbottom, the founder of the firm of Winterbottom (Wiredrawers) Ltd. was the son of Daniel Winterbottom, who was born in 1793 and died in 1848. George Winterbottom was one of six children, and was born in Barnsley in 1828.

He commenced his working life at the age of 12 years as an apprentice wiredrawer for a firm named Horsfalls, who, at that time had a mill betwen Market Hill and Graham's Orchard in Barnsley. Before reaching the age of 20 years, he was left in charge of the mill by Mr Horsfall, who went on a visit to America. On his return, Mr Horsfall gave him a letter commending him on looking after the works; this letter is still in existence.

George was married at the age of 24 years, and about this time left to work at a wire mill on the other side of the town in the Dearne Valley, a business owned by a family called Cockers; descendents of this firm are still in existence, running works in Sheffield. His stay at Cockers must have been of short duration, due to the fact that his family of five children were all born at Ringlinglow where he had become a partner in a firm producing wire. Records show that he was in partnership with a Mr Cook of Hathersage; this partnership was dissolved, and he took another partner by the name of Marsh. There are doubts as to how successful these associations were, as he finally left Ringinglow and came back to Barnsley to the previous firm of Horsfalls, where his sons William Jolley and Arthur Winterbottom were also employed.

It was during this time that William Jolley married Martha Walmsley, who was living and working in a shop near to the mill in Market Hill, Barnsley. They had five children, and these included all the recently retired Directors: George Arthur, Ernest William, Frank and Harry Austin Winterbottom.

George had a friendly association with the founder of Samuel Fox & Co. of Stocksbridge over a number of years, and discussed his problems with him. Mr Fox's offer to finance a new beginning was accepted, and a small mill was taken at Dodworth. The only stipulation made was that all wire which was drawn would be bought from Samuel Fox & Co.

*View of viaduct and engine, mill and house through arch*

George Winterbottom finally left Dodworth and came to Oxspring in 1888, bringing with him his family, including his sons and grandsons. The premises at Oxspring were taken on a lease, and were rented. From this time, they set about gathering established wiredrawers, and looking for outlets for wire, particularly in the Redditch area. It was in the year 1895 that C.F. Milward of Redditch were looking for a supply of wire for making into needle blanks, and in 1896 the association which continued until 1955 was confirmed, and the agreement signed. The value of the fittings at the time owned by George Winterbottom was assessed at £900, and to this Milwards added another £900, bringing the share capital between the two equal, the firm continuing to trade in the name of G. Winterbottom & Co.

The mill was then quite small, and was driven entirely by water power. A second-hand steam engine was purchased in 1896, and this was installed and worked successfully until 1954/5.

George Winterbottom died in 1905, and the control of the mill was passed to his sons William Jolley and Arthur Winterbottom. It would seem that the business thrived, since the outlet for wire, due to the association with Milwards, was assured. The firm increased in size very little from this time, due to the policy laid down by the Milward section of the company.

William Jolley died in 1926, and the control of the company was mainly in the hands of his sons and brother Arthur. It was at this period that Charles Milward (the son of the first partner) stipulated that the property should, if possible, be bought. Negotiations were conducted by George Wilby, Auctioneer and Valuer, who persuaded the executors of Thornley Taylor (the owner of the buildings and surrounding area) to sell the property. The outcome of this was that the mill was purchased outright, and became the sole property of Messrs G. Winterbottom & Co. Following this, the firm passed through a difficult period during the depression years, and it was not until 1936/7 that things began to improve; but from then until 1950 the factory was extremely busy.

Arthur Winterbottom died in the year 1947, when management affairs passed completely into the hands of George Arthur, Ernest William and Frank Winterbottom. This period saw a marked change in the Redditch Needle trade in that Milwards Fish Hooks had previously changed their name to The English Needle & Fishing Tackle Co. Ltd., and had begun to absorb still more needle manufacturers in Redditch. They changed their name yet again to Needle Industries Ltd., built a factory in Studley, and incorporated a new wiredrawing mill. This had a catastrophic effect on Winterbottom (Wiredrawers) Ltd. in that, on the occasion of the first recession after the war, there was insufficient work to keep both wire manufacturers busy. The outcome was that the Winterbottom section was left completely without work.

In the year 1953, the partnership was completely dissolved, whereupon three new Directors were incorporated: Harry Austin Winterbottom, S. Hinchliffe and Harold Marsh who, in addition to the three remaining brothers, G.A., E.W. and F. Winterbottom, began trading on a far more universal basis. Alterations in the processes of wire manufacturing were made, which increased the output, and lowered the cost of production. The steam engine was dismantled; electric power was installed; electric annealing took the place of the old bee-hive coal- fired annealing furnaces, and much progress was made.

*View from viaduct*

By the year 1963, prosperity had returned to the firm; outlets for material had increased one-hundredfold; and the Winterbottom reputation for good material was again established.

By 1970 Winterbottom (Wiredrawers) Ltd was becoming important to certain users, and it was considered by them, in order to safeguard their own supplies, prudent to suggest a merger. The offer was accepted from Eadie Bros. Holdings Ltd. of Paisley. However, the Company continued under the same management with little disruption but finally administered by the parent company. Development continues, and the Winterbottom name is well-known to most users of both stainless steel and carbon steel wire.

M. MARSH

*Mill*

The carved rock in Oxspring House Wood is in memory of the Rolling and Dransfield families. Rolling was the maiden name of John Ness Dransfield's mother, the only daughter of John Rolling of Oxspring corn mills.

*J.E. Dransfield stone*

# THURLSTONE

*Corn Mill*

## *Tenter Hill*

In earlier days the cloth trade had given employment to most of the Thurlstone people, working either at the mills or as weavers in their own homes. For this work there was a necessity to obtain as much daylight as possible; and so the weavers' cottages were built with an attic storey with as many windows as could be fitted. Several such rows of cottages still exist, of which Tenter Hill is a good example. The name of Tenter Hill derives from the tenters on which the finished cloth was stretched and dried. From this the expression, 'being on tenter hooks' arose.

*Tenter Hill*

*Corn Mill Corner, c.1910*

The first corn mill was built by Bosville in 1580, being rebuilt in 1761. In 1764 a court case took place between Amyor Rich of the corn mill and Waltons of the oil mill, over the use of water which worked the mill wheels. In 1917 the Penistone and District Farmers' Trading Society operated the mill. The mill was partly demolished in 1959 to reduce the bend in the road. The remainder was made into a house in 1970. The pictures show the mill as it was and as it is today.

*Corn Mill Corner today*

*Old Thurlstone from Rockside, c.1900.*

*Manchester Road, Thurlstone, as it was in 1910. The road on the right, now known as High Bank, was previously called 'Tallow Crap'. There the Greaves family, in a building on the left, boiled fat and dipped flax to make candles, the only form of lighting in the houses in the olden days.*

*Towngate, c.1900*

Towngate. On the left was Smithy Fold, the site of the birthplace of Nicholas Saunderson. The other picture shows it as it is at the present time.

*Towngate today*

*Old weaver's building, near Crystal Palace Hotel, Thurlstone, in 1965, showing weavers' windows on top floor. Note windows and doorway already built up below.*

*Manor House (Tudor cottage)*

The Tudor cottage was probably the manor house. One of the oldest buildings in Thurlstone, it is a typical Tudor building. On the right are weavers' cottages with their characteristic upper storey windows.

*Sunday School, 1786*

A Sunday School was opened in Penistone for the first time on Sunday, 28th February, 1813. Netherfield opened three years earlier, while the one pictured at Thurlstone started in 1786.

*Nicholas Saunderson stone at Thurlstone.* *(see text on page 34)*

*J.T. Smith's shop, c.1910*

## *J.T. Smith's*

J.T. Smith's shop in Thurlstone was founded in 1873. This photo was taken prior to 1911. It is thought that the man in the white apron was Mr Arnold Smith, with his brother Edgar alongside. The carters at that time were William Fretwell and Walter Crossland.

*Plumpton, c.1910*

*Plumpton today*

On the left of the picture dated c.1910 is Tomasson's cloth mill, founded in 1816, which became renowned for making livery cloth for the crowned heads of Europe. In 1929 the Wall Street Crash in America caused a slump in trade and the closure of the works in 1931. The other picture shows the present works, taken over by Durrans in 1936.

# GUNTHWAITE

*The Spa, today*

The Spa well at Gunthwaite is well known for the peculiar taste of its water and its reputed healing qualities, especially for scurvy and liver complaints. Spa Sunday is still celebrated annually on the first Sunday in May, when people come and drink the water.

It is said that in olden times thousands of people attended the festival, singing and dancing at the edge of the water, and were fed from stalls purposely erected and stocked with festive food.

The bridleway leading from the dam to Gunthwaite Hall and recorded in 1578, is an old packhorse way combining with the flag path above Cathill to make the track to Penistone.

*Bridle path today*

Gunthwaite barn, consisting of 11 bays, was built in the latter part of the sixteenth century and is 55 yds long, 15 yds wide, 30ft high (15ft to tie beams) and held together with wooden pegs. In the eighteenth century Mr John Wilson of Broomhead said that the doors were wide enough 'for a wain with six oxen to turn in it.'

The picture taken from the north side of the barn, shows the three large harr hung doors, presumably

## *Gunthwaite Barn*

*Barn from north side, 1987*

*Datestone and coat of arms over courthouse door, 1690*

adjacent to the three threshing floors. On the south side are several small doors with shaped wooden lintels.

The barn has been partitioned off inside, as the picture of the interior shows, and the beams with pegs and the massive 14″ x 9″ oak supports resting on large blocks of stone are a splendid sight.

## *Gunthwaite and the Bosvilles*

The name is of Saxon origin and an early deed gives the name William der Gunnilthwaite. Later in 1316 Roger de Gunthwaite was head of the family. He had a wife Isobel and a son John. John and his wife Christina took a tenement at Gunthwaite in 1348.

The Bosville family can be traced back to Sir Martin de Bosville in Normandy, who was treasurer to the army of William the Conqueror. Details of the family with the Gunthwaite pedigree are recorded in a book spanning nine centuries entitled *The Fortunes of a Family* by Lady Alice Macdonald of the Isles, published in 1928.

The most significant period in Gunthwaite history was during the life of the 3rd Godfrey Bosville and his wife Bridget, married in 1681 and commemorated in a stained glass window in Penistone Church which shows the arms of both families. The picture shows the Bosville coat of arms above the doorway in the stable block, with the initials GBB and date 1690 carved in the

*Barn interior, 1987*

stone lintel over the door. The other picture shows another similar carved stone in the gable end of an outbuilding, but with the date 1688.

Godfrey, known as Justice Bosville, was high sheriff of Yorkshire in 1705. The estate was sold to the tenant farmers in 1981.

*Datestone: B G B 1688*

The picture shows the only remains of the hall, demolished in the 19th century, or so it is related by the agent of the estate, named Earnshaw. The hall was built of stone below and black and white timber above, similar to the barn. Second hand timbers used to repair the mill structure may have come from the hall. The semi-circular projection on the left, with the window at ground level, could have contained a spiral staircase to the upper floor and perhaps a balcony. There are still beams in the ground floor ceiling carved with various crests.

The two-storey summer house complete with fireplaces and chimney, built in front of the hall, has been restored during recent years and the other picture shows the coat of arms and the ornate stone lintel with the familiar carving GBB 1688. The restored door replaces the original carved ones studded with great square nails.

*Gunthwaite, 1987*

*Summer house*

*Summer house door*

*Oak*

The remains of the giant oak tree in the garden behind the hall is said to be the grave of a large number of Cromwell's men who died in an epidemic. In its prime it was 36ft in diameter. The stable block built by Godfrey can be seen behind the tree.

It is recorded (c. 1360) as a glorious tree in the days of Thomas Bosville of Ardsley and his wife Alicia, who was the daughter of John de Gunthwaite.

## *Gunthwaite Mill*

Gunthwaite Mill has been part of the Bosville Estate since medieval times, and ceased grinding corn for the local farmers in 1956. To keep the mill working during the Second World War, hawthorn from the farm was used to repair the cog wheels. The mill is mentioned in 1348, and with the name of Thomas de Bosseville de Erdesley in 1359. In 1731 the cost of building the house at the mill was £15.17s.

*Oatmeal kiln*

*Mill water wheel*

The waterwheel shown is 20ft dia and some 4ft wide, with 48 buckets. The hearth, complete with iron doors, is the kiln for drying oats. The oats were laid on the floor above the hearth and when dry were ground to make oatmeal. On the picture of the mill interior is a general view of the grinding floor. There are three sets of stones. The large pinion and lineshaft are made of iron but the rest, including the bevel gears, pulleys and bearings, are of hardwood. On this floor is the belt-driven unit (with the maker's name, 'Jones Wire Works, Leeds') used for sifting the flour. On the floor below is the gearing and drive shafts for the stones, and the chutes and troughs for the finished flour and meal.

*Mill Interior*

*Broad Oak Tree*

The tree is of similar age and size to its near neighbour, the great oak at Gunthwaite Hall, and gave Broad Oak Farm its name. The farm was bought from the Hawksworth family in 1720 (so completing the Bosville Estate) by William, heir to his uncle, Godfrey.

# WATER HALL

*Water Hall, c.1900; on left of the crossroads is the old toll bar, the houses called Viewlands not yet built.*

*Water Hall, c.1915 (Viewlands erected, 1914)*

*Water Hall, 1930's; development of houses taking place.*

*Water Hall, 1987; toll bar demolished 1934.*

*Water Hall, c.1900*

In 1379 the poll tax returns mentions 'Ricardus atte Water Hall', which is the earliest record of the area. A deed executed at Penistone in 1392 was witnessed by one Nicholas Wordsworth, and it was the ancient home of the Wordsworth family for many years, having connections with the poet William Wordsworth. A place of historical interest, it has been modernized in the past few years and much of the land is now housing estates.

*Pack Horse Bridge. The picture shows the original pack horse bridge on the right. This bridle path led to the manor court at Gunthwaite in Tudor and Stuart times. It collapsed in 1944 and was rebuilt in 1946.*

# NETHER MILL

*Corn Mill, c.1910*

*Mill from goyt*

*W.H. Hinchliff's corn mill at Bridge End was built on the site of a former mill which was destroyed by fire. It is believed to have been a mill site for at least two centuries. It was demolished in June 1961 to make way for road development.*

# PUBLIC HOUSES

*New Inn. In use in 1850, it is now almost derelict. It stands in a field on the north side of the Scout Dyke end of the Penistone by-pass (the A629).*

*Prince of Wales. Situated at 90 High Street, it is now Wiseman's Provision Merchants, who commenced business c.1860. The founder was Mr Lancelot Burdett, great grandfather of Robert Wiseman.*

*White Bear , closed 26th December 1925, was later the British Legion Club, now part of A.M. Clark's chemist's.*

*Horns Inn. This was first a coffee house and tavern and later O. Wood's, butchers, followed by William Marsden's butchers. It is now an estate agent's. The sign 'Bentley's Beers' can still be seen at the top of the front of the building.*

*Fleece Inn. Kept by Joshua Mosley (1775) and later his son, William (1882). They were also clockmakers, and many of their clocks can still be seen locally. Today the premises, 29 Market Street, are occupied by Shirley Anne Hairstylist and Cherrytree Chinese Takeaway.*

*Railway Tavern. Built to serve the old railway station which was adjacent in Bridge Street. It was replaced by the Wentworth Arms when the railway station was moved to its new site.*

# SPORTS

**Penistone Juniors football team, 1930-31**

**Back row:** W. Julian, A.R. Lee, C. Taylor, W. Upton, H. Mackenzie,
**Front row:** A.E. Brownhill, G. Bashforth, H. Faxon, F. Caffrey, H. Moorhouse, H. Crossland

**Penistone(?) Rugby Club, 1892.** Unfortunately very little is known of the history of this club to date.

**Back row:** R. Hoskins, J. Rolling
**3rd row:** Z. Tinker, F. Langley, W. Latimer, G. Brownhill, W. Fieldsend, Calcutt, Eastwood
**2nd row:** Wainwright, T. Armitage, ----- , J. King, T. Oates, D. Roberts
**Front:** A. Hadfield

**Penistone St John's School Cricket Team, 1930 (Winners of the Penistone and District Shield)**

**Back row:** H. Inchley, S. Roebuck, M. Roebuck
**Centre row:** Wood, E. Foster, H. Brooks, Fillingham, G. Fowler, G. Sewell, J. Wood, Wood
**Front row:** C. Walsh, J. Swift, D. Wade, J. Birkinshaw, G. Healey, W. Hinchliff

## *Penistone Hunt*

The Penistone Hunt with masters, dating back to Elias de Midhope in 1260, is now, alas, one of the many things of the past. It finally disappeared during the second world war when feeding difficulties closed the kennels at Cathill. The hounds were at one time kept by members in their homes, who would bring them together when a 'meet' occurred.

**Penistone and District Bowling Club, c.1961**

**Back row:** J. Broadhead, S. Dyson, R. Littlewood, R. Langley, A. Horsfield, J. Cope, J. Marsden, S. Palmer,
**Centre row:** S. Crownshaw, F. Marsden, J. Taylor, L. Burgin, W. Webster, H. Jagger, W. Brearley, H. Field, Sparling
**Front row:** T. Lodge, J.T. Biltcliffe, S. Platt, D. Hinchliffe, H. Watkinson, J. Champion, W. Chapel, S. Denton, G. Carr

**Four veteran bowlers (total age of 330 years) in 1945**

A. Benson (82), J. Peace (90), R.H. Julian (78), H. Mellor (80)

## 1984 winners of the Sheffield Parks Ellse League

**Back row:** T. Wilkinson, C. Latimer, W. Atkinson, R.N. Brownhill, W. Davenport
**Front row:** C. Stead, L. Maude, M. Jagger, G. Beever, A. Walshaw

The Penistone and District bowling green was opened on 29th April 1909

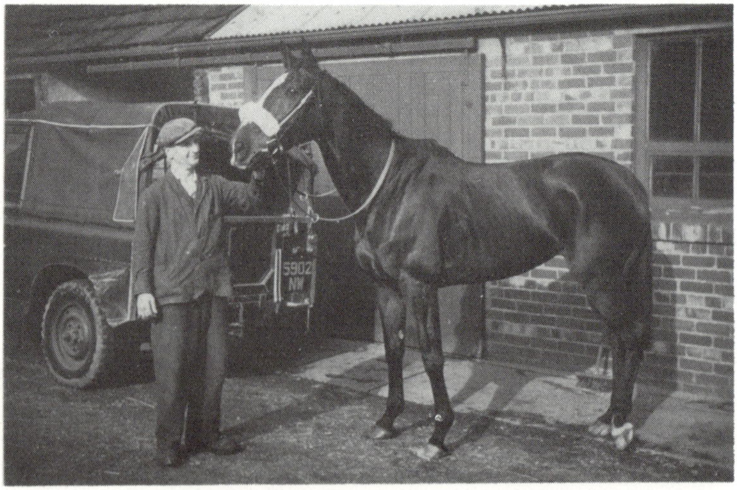

*'Happy Dene' with racehorse owner and trainer the late Mr George Stanley at Cathill Farm, Hoylandswaine, in 1959.*

Horse racing was held at Racecommon, Penistone, between 1726 and 1730. In 1726 Mr Garforth, Minister of Midhope Chapel, won the plate, while in 1728 on 1st August the plate, £3, was won by a horse from Lancashire.

**Thurlstone Handbell Ringers, English Championship Winners 1930**

**Back Row:** L. Sykes, C. Mitchell, N. Crossland, M. Walshaw, E. Wood
**Front Row:** T. Sykes, M. Beard, R. Lees, F. Taylor, C. Latimer, H. Beard, J. Beever

**Thurlstone Bell Orchestra:** *photograph taken by Mr B. Rolling in 1983 at Cubley Brook (signature tune)*

Thurlstone Handbell Ringers were formed in 1855. They won the Yorkshire Handbell Ringers Association Shield & Cup in 1930, 1931 and 1932. The name was changed c.1970. Mr A. Dyson has been the conductor since 1967. In 1900 a set of bells cost approx £180. The present day cost would be £15/16,000.

**Back Row:** H. Gill, A. Rolling, C. Armitage, S. Rolling, A. Dyson, G. Beever, B. Beever, D. Moseley
**Front Row:** D. Hague, B. Hague, M. Watts, J. Mathews, B. Rolling

## *Thurlstone Brass Band*

The band was formed in 1854. Previous conductors include Messrs A. Staniforth, H. Green, W. Hampshire and E. Foster. In 1904 the band competed at the Crystal Palace, London, and came first in the Preliminary Cup. Mr E. Crossley, the immediate past conductor, held the post of musical director from 1954. The band's performance in 1978, when it entered six contests and was successful in all of them, is a typical example of the standard achieved and consistently maintained.

## *Penistone Show*

The Penistone Agricultural Society, established in 1853, staged its 115th Show this year, 1987, it having lapsed for a few years during the two world wars etc.

The Show was first held in the ground behind the Town Hall on a Thursday, market day. 1883 saw a change of venue, moving to Brickfield, Unwin Street, and also a change of day to Saturday. These changes and a wet day finished the show until 1889, when it was revived and held on a Thursday on Baileys Park, which is now Park Avenue estate. In 1895 it returned to its original site behind the Town Hall, where it remained until 1948. In 1949 it again moved, this time to Water Hall, finally moving to its present site on Stottercliffe.

# LANDMARKS

Hartcliffe Tower, a folly built in 1856 by H. Richardson, a linen merchant who later became the first Mayor of Barnsley, was a fine vantage point from which to view Penistone and district. Sadly it is now unsafe to climb, and is also out of bounds to the visitor. Situated at the entrance to the field in which it stands is an old milestone.

*Hartcliffe Tower and Guide Post*

*Cross or guide post*

Set in a field on the left hand side of the road to Hartcliffe is another cross, said by some to have been the Penisale Market Cross erected by Richard Lovetot (c. 1134), but by others to have been only a guide for travellers over what was formerly part of the open moor.

The summer house at Hartcliffe, another folly built at the same time as the tower in 1856 by H. Richardson, commanded one of the finest views of the district. It was sadly blown down in December 1964 after being a prominent landmark of Penistone for over one hundred years.

*Hartcliffe Summer House*

*Milestone*

The old stone in the picture can be found just over the wall at the crossroads at the top of Underbank, on the road from Penistone to Stocksbridge. A directional stone dated 1734, it indicates the routes of the old pack horse roads. The Sheffield-Manchester-Halifax turnpike road passed through this point and a road from Birdwell also joined it, while yet another route crossed the main Rotherham-Manchester road at Howbrook, continuing from Wortley down Finkle Street and over Green Moor towards the Manchester road over Woodhead. In 1940, with the threat of invasion becoming a reality, all the country's milestones and signposts were dismantled, this one being dug up and buried. It was not until some 44 years later that a local farmer, after much searching, found it and restored it to its former site.

*Greyhound Stone*

The Greyhound Stone in the wall near Belle Vista on the right hand side of the road leading to Hartcliffe, a boundary stone with a figure of a greyhound upon it. It is mentioned in the survey of the old boundaries of Langsett and Thurlstone in 1695, and may have marked the boundary of the Lordship of Hallamshire. Thomas Lord Furnival paid on the feast of St John the Baptist, as quit for this Lordship, two white greyhounds annually to the King. The letters MWP may refer to Lord Melbourne and William Payne, both owners of a large estate in the township of Langsett.

*Take Off Stone*

Situated on the Penistone-Midhope road, on the south side of Cranberry crossroads, in the wall on the right is the Take Off Stone marking the place where extra horses, used to help pull heavy loads up Sheephouse Height, were unhitched.

Boulder Bridge at Spring Vale can claim great antiquity. An extract from the January 1978 edition of *The Bridge*, the church magazine, stated that on 12th January 1495, as he lay dying, Father William Wordsworth (Vicar of Penistone for 40 years) gave 12 silver pieces to build a bridge called 'Bulder Brig'.

*Boulder Bridge*

Built c.1734 as a pack horse bridge, Willow Bridge bore people and their horses etc. over the Don on the way to the mediaeval market at Wakefield. It can be found by the visitor by following the lane opposite St Aidan's Church, Oxspring.

*Willow Bridge, Oxspring*

The Four Lane Ends at Oxspring is the place where stands the Travellers Inn, featured in Phyllis Crossland's book *Years of Grace* (Bridge Publications, 1985). Photographed c. 1895. The other picture shows the Travellers Inn as it is today.

*Cliff Cottage, Hoylandswaine*

The picture shows a flagstone at Cliff Cottage on Hoylandswaine Heights. It is said that fifteen churches can be seen from here.

The unusual stone council notice is at the side of a farm road on the south side of Ingbirchworth.

*Traction Engine Stone, Ingbirchworth*

# SOCIETIES

The Penistone Charitable Society was formed in 1763 and was still in existence in 1821. In 1812 the quarterly subscription was 2s. 6d. One of the qualifications for membership was 'that no regular soldier, seafaring man, miner or member of any other charitable society or any person under the age of 18 and above that of 30 years can be admitted a member of this society, except as a free member'. Relief varied according to years of membership, ranging from 5s. 0d. per week to 8s. 0d. per week for the first 12 weeks, then reduced by half for the remainder of the illness. Rule 10 shows some of the restrictions to claiming benefit.

*Rule 10: Penistone Charitable Society*

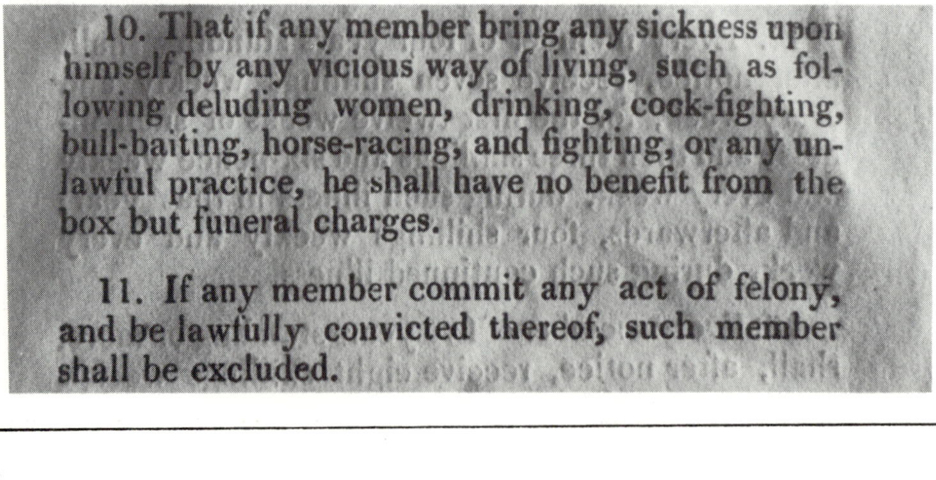

10. That if any member bring any sickness upon himself by any vicious way of living, such as following deluding women, drinking, cock-fighting, bull-baiting, horse-racing, and fighting, or any unlawful practice, he shall have no benefit from the box but funeral charges.

11. If any member commit any act of felony, and be lawfully convicted thereof, such member shall be excluded.

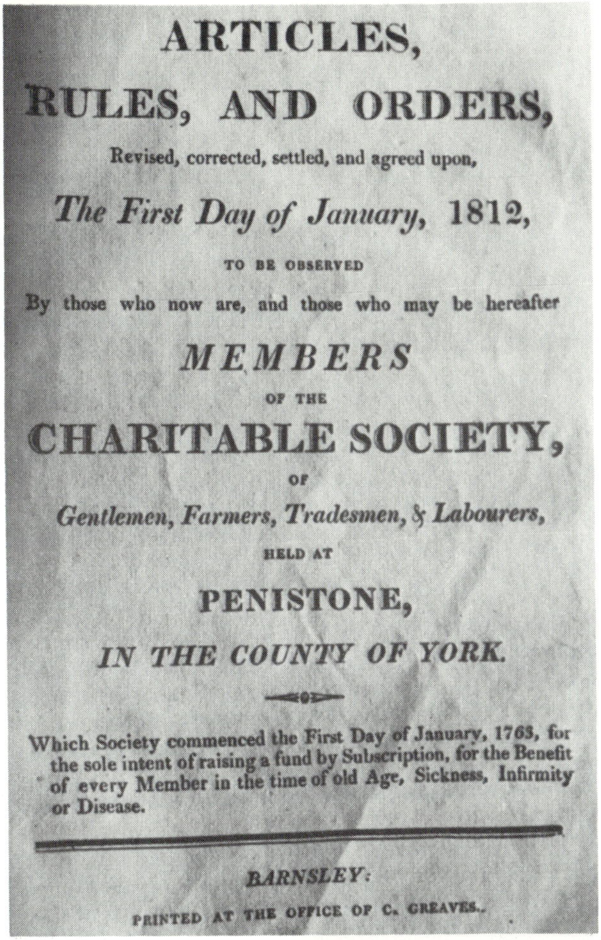

ARTICLES,
RULES, AND ORDERS,
Revised, corrected, settled, and agreed upon,
*The First Day of January*, 1812,
TO BE OBSERVED
By those who now are, and those who may be hereafter
*MEMBERS*
OF THE
CHARITABLE SOCIETY,
OF
*Gentlemen, Farmers, Tradesmen, & Labourers,*
HELD AT
PENISTONE,
*IN THE COUNTY OF YORK.*

Which Society commenced the First Day of January, 1763, for the sole intent of raising a fund by Subscription, for the Benefit of every Member in the time of old Age, Sickness, Infirmity or Disease.

*BARNSLEY:*
PRINTED AT THE OFFICE OF C. GREAVES.

*Thurlstone Building Society, 1799*

The Thurlstone Building Society was formed on 6th April 1799 and there are 19 signatures on the deed. There were two grades of houses, namely £100 and £50 with deposits and quarterly repayments of £1.1s.0d. and 10s.6d. and 26s.0d. and 13s.0d. respectively. At meetings a fine of 2s.6d. was levied for abusive language, refusing to be silent, or being drunk, with a maximum of 3d. to be spent on liquor. The Penistone and Thurlstone Building Society was established in 1867 with the President Revd W.S. Turnbull. It was subsequently amalgamated into the Leek & Westbourne, later becoming part of the Britannia Building Society.

The Articles
Whereas
First
Sixth
Seventh
Eighth
Ninth
Tenth

# CLOCKS

*Joseph Mosley Clock*

The clock on the left and top of the page was made by Joseph Mosley of Penistone. The corner spandrels suggest a date of between 1760 and 1780 and are of a design called Castle Gateway. The clock is owned by D.W. Roebuck of Penistone, who in 1961 bought the works from a scrap dealer for £1. Unfortunately the case had been destroyed, as at the time it was regarded as of little value. In 1964, in his search for a case, Mr Roebuck discovered a centre portion that was being used as a cocktail cabinet. He purchased this for £1.50, leaving only the bottom section missing, this finally being made by B. Cartwright of Millhouse from an old oak bedstead. The clock was then assembled and the clock works set in motion by Arthur Champion. The clock and chimes work perfectly at the present time, some 200 years after being made. It is interesting to note that the second hand travels anti-clockwise.

*Joseph Mosley Clock*

*Joshua Mosley Clock*

Another clock made by the Mosley family, with the signature 'Joshua Mosley Peniston'. The spandrels named String of Pearls date it again as being between 1760 and 1780. It is owned by a Penistone businessman, being found by accident in a Sheffield antique shop. The case and clock are believed to be original, the works and chimes again function perfectly.

# CLIMATE

Three unusually heavy falls of snow have occurred in Penistone in living memory. These were in 1933, 1947 and 1963. The heaviest, in 1933, is recorded in the two pictures of High Street and Church Hill. The young man digging in the High Street is Gordon Heeley, son of the shoe repairer.

*High Street Snow, 1933*

*Church Hill, 1933*

# GENERAL

*Whit Walk 1933, Thurlstone*

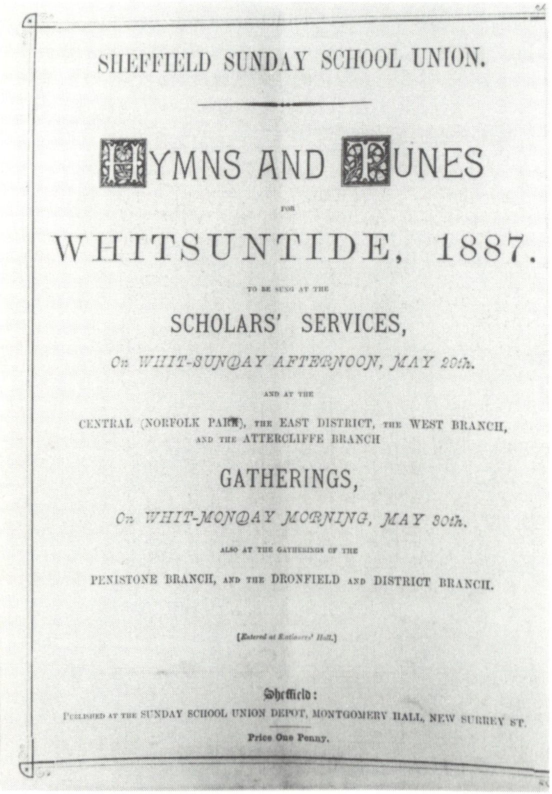

SHEFFIELD SUNDAY SCHOOL UNION.

HYMNS AND TUNES

FOR

WHITSUNTIDE, 1887.

TO BE SUNG AT THE

SCHOLARS' SERVICES,

*On WHIT-SUNDAY AFTERNOON, MAY 29th.*

AND AT THE

CENTRAL (NORFOLK PARK), THE EAST DISTRICT, THE WEST BRANCH, AND THE ATTERCLIFFE BRANCH

GATHERINGS,

*On WHIT-MONDAY MORNING, MAY 30th.*

ALSO AT THE GATHERINGS OF THE

PENISTONE BRANCH, AND THE DRONFIELD AND DISTRICT BRANCH.

[*Entered at Stationers' Hall.*]

Sheffield:

PUBLISHED AT THE SUNDAY SCHOOL UNION DEPOT, MONTGOMERY HALL, NEW SURREY ST.

Price One Penny.

*Whit Programme, 1887*

## *Whit Walks*

The Whitsuntide walks date back to 1867. As the photograph shows, it was then part of the Sheffield Sunday School Union.

On the 73rd programme of 1940 its title had been changed to Penistone & Thurlstone Sunday School Union. Many photographs are in existence, taken annually, and the various groups could be seen along with Penistone Grammar School form photos in the windows of the shop in Bridge Street as seen on page 21.

In 1987 the walk was replaced by a Pentecost Praise Service in the Parish Church.

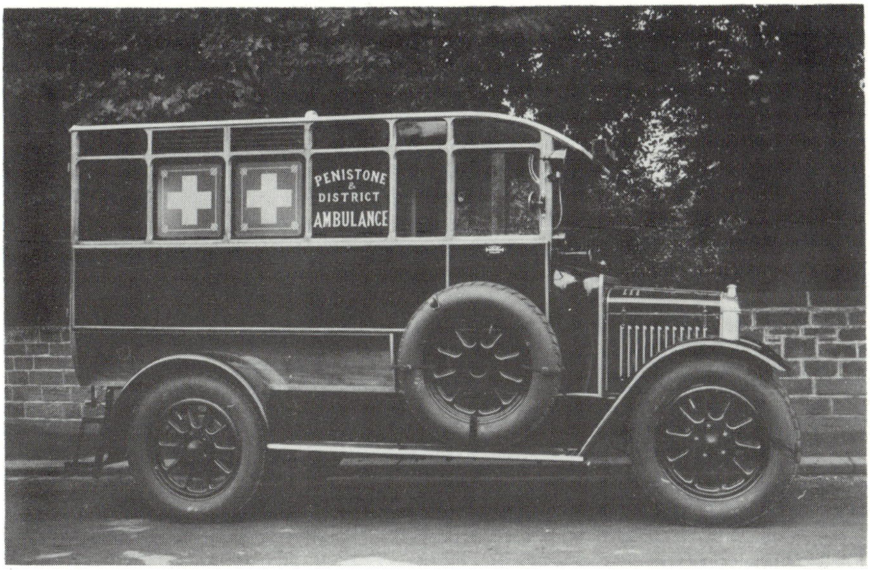


*Penistone Ambulance, c.1927*

*Flood at Brown's*

The flood at Green Road was caused by heavy rainfall and the subsequent blocking of the culvert, c.1956.

*Nailmakers' shops, Hoylandswaine*

The nailmakers' workshops were replaced by the almshouses at Hoylandswaine in 1906. They were built by Alderman George Senior, who was Lord Mayor of Sheffield. He was born in Bradfield, lived in Hoylandswaine for 13 years, and helped his father to make nails.

*Now Almshouses*

*Alf Chappell*

Nailmaking, using locally made iron (probably from Wortley Forge), has been a craft in Hoylandswaine for many years. In the Hoylandswaine Militia Returns of 1806 there were recorded the names and ages of 20 nailmakers. Mr Alf Chappell, seen on the left, was one of the last local craftsmen. It is not known if he worked in one of the buildings pictured or in the three workshops still to be seen on the roadside above the Lord Nelson Inn. The hearth and bellows in one shop were still intact in 1965.

The Penistone breed of sheep was to be found on the borders of Yorkshire, Lancashire and Derbyshire. They were named 'Penistone' after the town in which they were sold. A few still remain today. They have white faces and legs, and both rams and ewes have large horns, and rather long tails.

*Penistone Sheep*

*Wood's Original Garage*

*Penney's Garage*

Oxspring Garage (above) was originally a blacksmith's shop, established about 1920 by Mr Hewitt and constructed of wood. As can be seen in the picture, it was situated in front of the existing building which replaced it in 1960. In 1926 the late Jim Wood took over the blacksmith's and changed it into a garage. In 1985 his son Gordon, the present owner, won 1st prize in a petrol company's nationwide top station competition with over 600 garages competing.

Spring Vale Garage, still in existence, was founded in 1924 by Cecil Penney, who previously worked for William Gittus & Son. The picture with Mrs Penney standing at the side of the one and only petrol pump shows the garage in 1925. The later picture, taken in 1936, shows 6 pumps selling different brands of petrol, namely: Cleveland Discol, National Benzole, Esso, Esso Ethyl, Power and B.P.

# CHURCH TOWER VIEWS

*Viewlands, 1976. The old Penistone show ground in the middle of the picture is now completely filled in with houses.*

*Netherfield, 1976. Nothing much has changed.*

*Viaduct, 1976*

*Market area, showing present showground area.*